# mini DESIGNERS

# mini DESIGNERS

## 20 projects inspired by the great designers

Joséphine Seblon

illustrated by Robert Sae-Heng

# Contents

6   Introduction

8   How to use this book

mini
DESIGNERS OF THE PAST

12   Shining decorations
Ancient Greek brooch

16   Patterned tiles
Roman mosaic flooring

20   Celebration lights
Chinese paper lanterns

24   Illustrated initials
Medieval illuminated manuscripts

28   Pinched clay pots
Japanese raku pottery

32   Printed paper
William Morris's patterned wallpaper

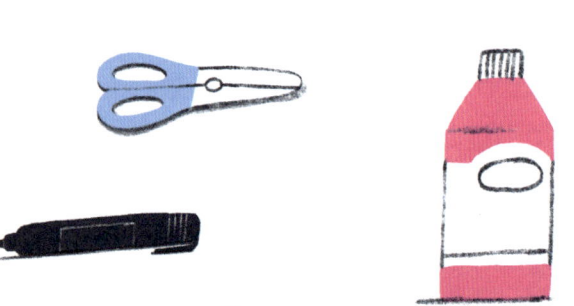

## mini
## MODERN DESIGNERS

**38  Fantastical cities**
London Underground map

**42  Lollipop loungers**
Marsan lounge chair

**46  Mini motorcars**
Ferrari racing car

**50  Hanging mobile**
Bruno Munari's *Useless Machines*

**54  Split pin puppets**
Charles and Ray Eames' *Colouring Toy*

**58  Eye-catching images**
*Children Crossing* road sign

**62  Overlapping letters**
Massimo Vignelli's typography posters

## mini
## CONTEMPORARY DESIGNERS

**68  Pixel art creatures**
Susan Kare's Dogcow

**72  Stylish tea set**
Marimekko's bold patterns

**76  Patchwork jars**
Hella Jongerius' mixed-media vases

**80  Recycled tower**
Brunno Jahara's fruit stands

**84  Yarn coasters**
Simone Post's recycled fabric creations

**88  Super stools**
Jean-Servais Somian's basin seats

**92  Joyful pavements**
Yinka Ilori's colourful murals

**96  List of designs**

# 'Everything is design.
# Everything!'

PAUL RAND

After creating and testing craft projects for *Mini Artists* and *Mini Architects* with my children over the last few years, I wondered what the next step in our creative journey might be. Looking around my home, I noticed many objects: vases, chairs, book covers, dishes, toys. I saw my children: one was playing with some cardboard food we made together and the other was drawing a poster for a birthday party. I realised I had two mini designers right before my eyes.

As with buildings, but unlike artworks, designed products have a purpose: a practical function complemented by aesthetic form. It is an easy concept for children – who see and use these products every day – to understand.

But what can mini designers learn from the great designers?

Looking at various objects, products and graphics from ancient times to the present day, mini designers will learn that good design has many benefits. It provides efficient solutions to life's challenges and can be an empowering and effective way for children to make their voices heard in today's world.

This book is here to help mini designers learn that simplicity is often the key to success, that limitations can stimulate creativity, that colours have meaning and that nature is a constant source of inspiration.

Joséphine Seblon

Charles and Ray Eames, *The Toy*, 1951

# How to use this book

## Build a craft box

Each project lists the items you will need, but it is helpful to have extra materials to hand for when you're feeling creative. Build a craft box with the essentials: white and coloured paper, pencils and pens, washable and watercolour paints, modelling clay, glue and scissors, a ruler and plenty of recycled materials waiting for a new life!

## Pick the right project

Each project in this book is unique. Some are suitable for very young children (those involving clay or printing, for instance), others require more advanced skills or attention to detail. Keep in mind your mini designers' interests and tastes. Are they into video games? Make some pixel art creatures (p. 68). Or if they enjoy acting, create some puppet characters (p. 54). There is something for everyone!

## Discover different techniques

Design has many facets and uses a wide range of techniques. Work with your mini designers to explore various techniques and mediums, from potato printing to scrape painting, from embossing to hand-lettering. Observe which techniques they enjoy, but encourage them to step out of their comfort zones and try new things.

## Make it your own

Mini designers will be inspired by some of the best designers in history, but these projects are not intended to perfectly mimic their styles. The instructions are a starting point to get ideas flowing. Borrow tips from other projects to make each piece unique. What would a potato print road sign or a flower-patterned racing car look like?

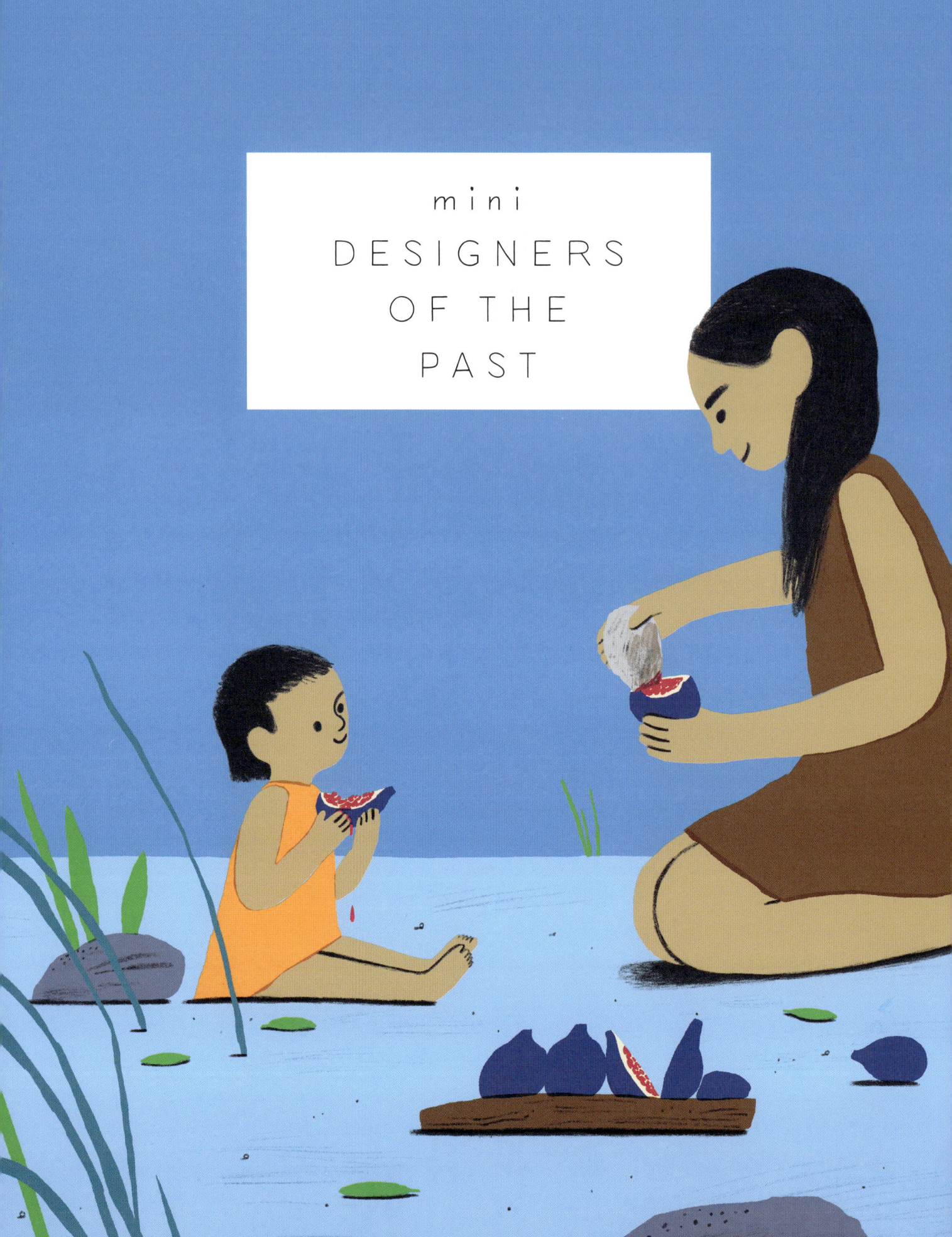

mini
DESIGNERS
OF THE
PAST

The first human-made tool we know about was a rock carved into a teardrop shape. It was made about 500,000 years ago and was used to cut and prepare food. Ever since then, people have been designing useful tools and interesting objects.

Mini designers will discover how ancient Romans covered floors with mosaics and Victorians covered walls with patterned paper. They will learn how Japanese pottery makers and medieval scribes made their wares special and unique. Every project in this section is full of beauty and colour.

# Shining decorations

Ancient Greek brooch

## Look at this!

Look at this gold brooch. Can you see the head framed by the sun's rays? It's Helios, the ancient Greek god of the sun. Gold was a very precious material in ancient Greece, and it still is today. Gold is a soft metal, which makes it easy to shape into a design, and its shiny colour makes it the perfect material to represent the sun, don't you think?

Hellenistic Helios medallion-brooch, c. 400-300 BCE

## Discuss this!

When you hammer a pattern into metal, it is called 'embossing'. This technique creates a 3D design, and it takes a lot of skill.

• Can you think of any other metals that could be used to make jewellery? Have you heard of silver or copper?

• The sun and the crescent moon were popular pendant shapes in ancient Greece. Does anyone you know own a brooch or a pendant? What shapes do they have?

• Some ancient jewellery was made to look like plants or animals. What shapes from nature would you like to wear?

# Give it a go!

It's your turn to make some hanging golden decorations.

## You will need:

- Empty tomato purée tube (or sheet of gold foil)
- Scissors
- Tea towel
- Metal spoon
- Thin paintbrush
- String or ribbon

1

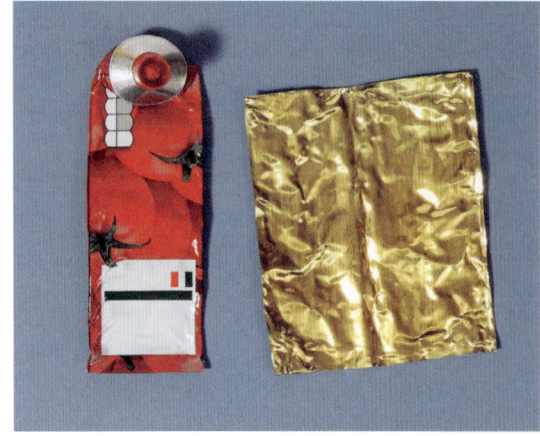

Ask an adult to cut off the top and bottom of the empty tomato purée tube, and cut down one side of the tube to open it up into a sheet. Wash the sheet to reveal the golden insides (be careful, the edges of the tube can be sharp).

2

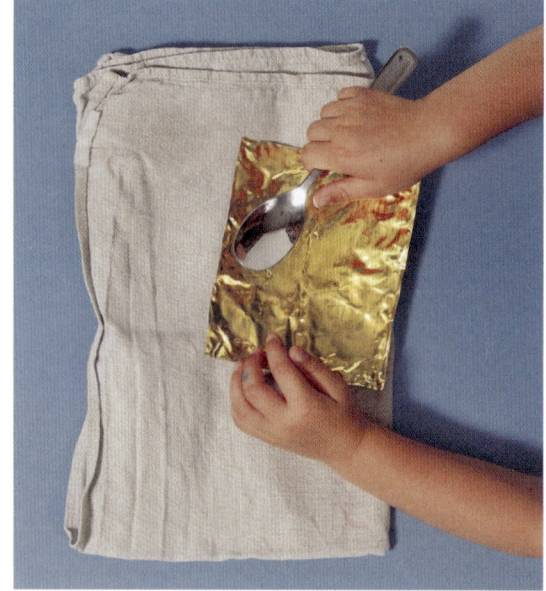

Put the sheet on top of a tea towel, with the gold side facing up. Make the sheet smooth by firmly pressing and rubbing the back of a spoon over it.

3

Turn the gold sheet over. Press the outline of a crescent moon shape into the metal with the tip of a paintbrush handle.

4

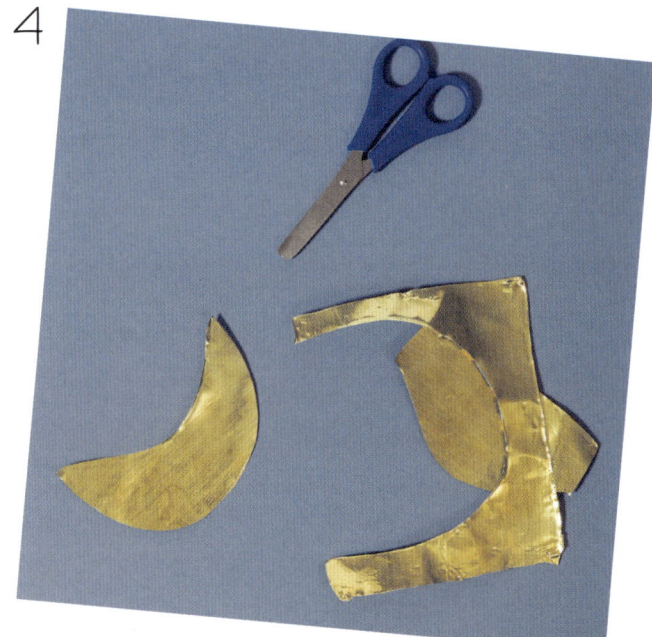

Ask an adult to help cut out your decoration, using a pair of scissors.

Top tip! If you aren't happy with your lines, turn the metal sheet over to the gold side and erase the lines with the back of a spoon.

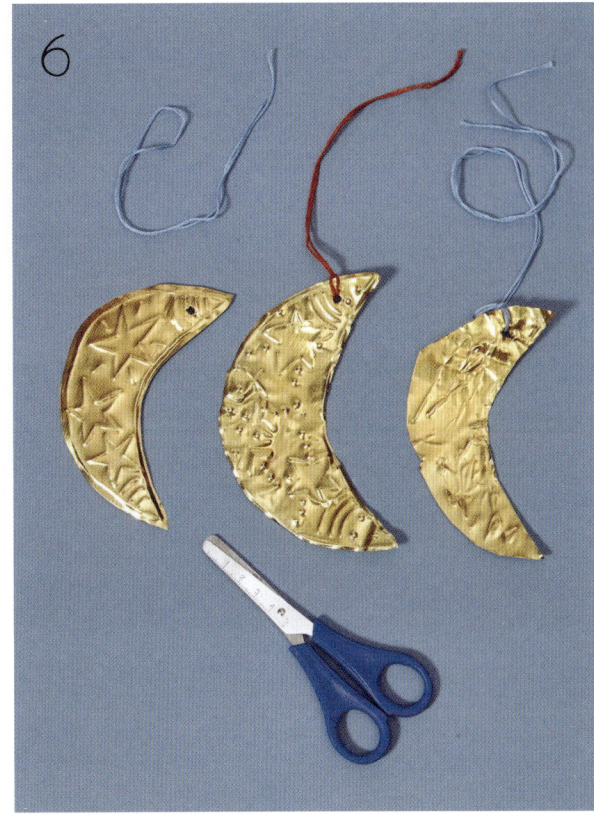

Turn your decoration over. Use the paintbrush handle to press your patterns into the metal, such as dots, swirls and zig-zags. When you turn it over to the gold side, you should see the patterns sticking out.

Ask an adult to pierce a small hole in the top of the decoration with a pair of scissors. Thread a piece of string or ribbon through the hole and tie the ends together to make a loop. Now hang up your shining decoration.

# Try this!

If you like working with metal, why not make Hojalata - or Mexican Tin? You will need a roll of aluminium foil, a spoon and coloured marker pens. Tear a sheet of foil and press a design into the dull side of the foil, using the tip of a fork handle. Then turn the foil over to the shiny side and decorate your design with coloured felt-tip pens.

# Patterned tiles

Roman mosaic flooring

## Look at this!

Roman mosaic, Spoleto, Italy, c. 1st century CE

Rich people in ancient Rome decorated the floors of their villas – big houses – with small coloured tiles called tesserae. The tiles were arranged to make pictures called mosaics. Wave patterns like this one were often used to make borders around the edges of the floors.

## Discuss this!

Different kinds of rooms in ancient villas would have different mosaic designs. Hallways had simple patterns and guest rooms had more complicated pictures.

• Look at the wave design. Can you imagine the waves on the sea? What would they sound like?

• What sort of room do you think this wave pattern would be found in? Where would you put it in your home?

• Do you have any tiles in your home? What rooms are they in? Are they on the walls or the floor?

## Give it a go!

Have a go at making some bean and seed mosaics.

## You will need:

- White, air-dry clay
- Rolling pin
- Modelling tools (or a butter knife)
- Small bowl of water (for wetting the clay and cleaning fingers)
- Dried beans, seeds and lentils
- Tracing paper and a pencil (optional)

1

Use a rolling pin to roll the air-dry clay into a square, about 1 cm thick.

2

Choose a shape for your design. What about a fish or a butterfly? Use a modelling knife to cut the shape out of the clay.

3

Use your fingertips to make the edges of your shape smooth. If the clay is too dry, wet your fingertips with a little water.

4

Firmly push dried beans, seeds and lentils into your clay shape to make a pattern.

5

6

When you are happy with your pattern, roll the rolling pin over your shape to firmly stick the beans, seeds and lentils in place.

Leave your shape on a flat surface in a warm, dry place, such as a windowsill or high shelf, for around 2-3 days until the clay hardens.

**Top tip!** Draw your shape on a piece of tracing paper first, then use the paper to trace the shape onto the clay before you cut it out.

## Try this!

Make a mosaic design out of pebbles. Find pebbles with interesting shapes and colours. Wash and dry them, then arrange them on a piece of paper to make a picture. When you are happy, glue the pebbles onto the paper. Why not make an owl – the symbol of wisdom in ancient Rome?

# Celebration lights

## Chinese paper lanterns

Look at this!

If you visit China at New Year, you're sure to see lots of paper lanterns like this one. They are made of thin, red paper and come in lots of shapes and sizes. On the final day of Chinese New Year celebrations, there is a lantern festival where children light the night with paper lanterns to welcome in a new year full of good fortune.

Chinese paper lantern

## Discuss this!

Paper lanterns – or Dēnglóng in Chinese – were used over 2,000 years ago, way before electricity!

• Do you have any lampshades in your home? What shapes are they?

• In Chinese culture, the colour red represents good fortune. Can you guess what yellow and green represent (answer below)?

• What other decorations are used for celebrations or holidays? What are your favourite celebration decorations?

Answers: yellow represents royalty and green represents harmony.

# Give it a go!

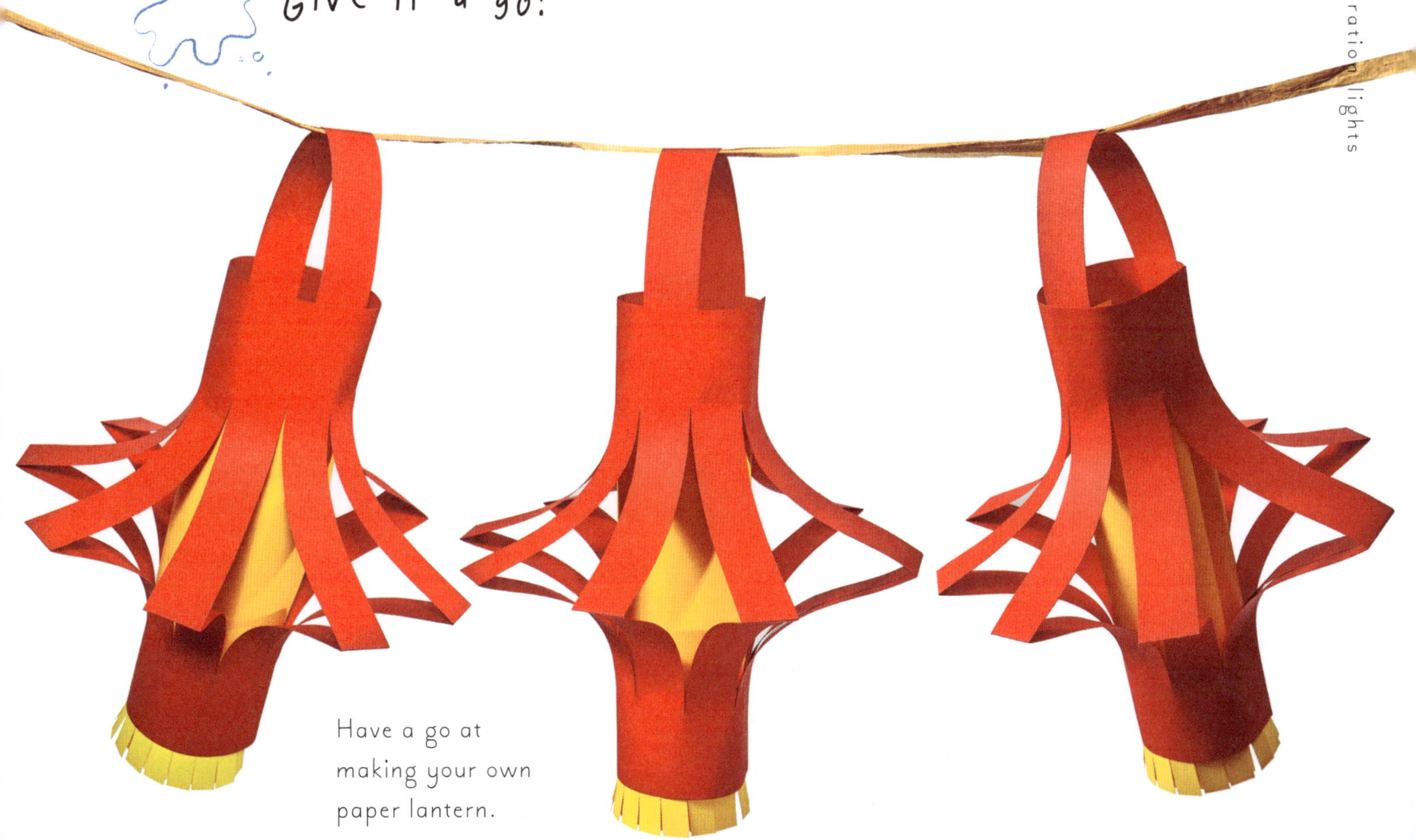

Have a go at making your own paper lantern.

## You will need:

· Red and yellow paper
· Scissors
· Double-sided tape

1

Fold your sheet of red paper in half width-ways.

2

Use scissors to cut straight lines through the folded edge of the paper, stopping 3 cm from the opposite edge. Space each cut about 1.5 cm apart.

3

Unfold the paper and bring the long sides together to make a tube shape. Attach the long sides together with double-sided tape.

4

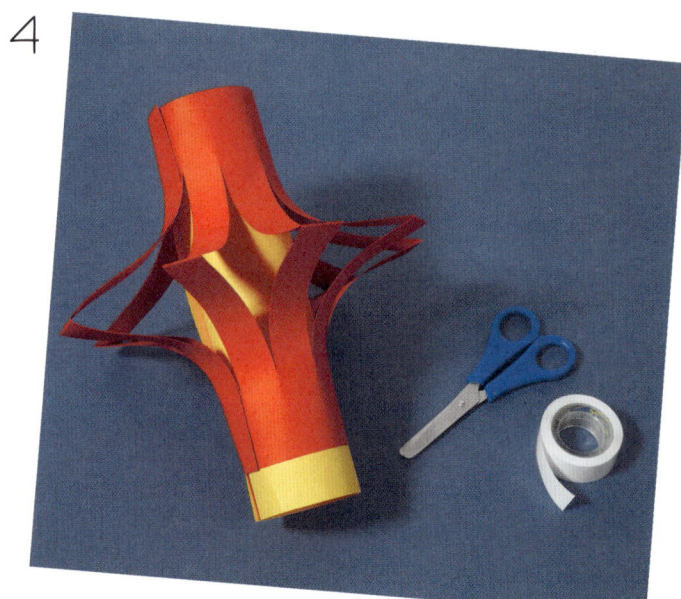

Roll the yellow paper into a long tube shape. Slide the yellow tube inside the red tube, but not all the way. Make sure 2 cm of yellow paper sticks out of the bottom of the red tube. Use double-sided tape to stick the yellow tube in place.

Top tip!    Write a message on a piece of paper and attach it to your lantern for people to read.

5

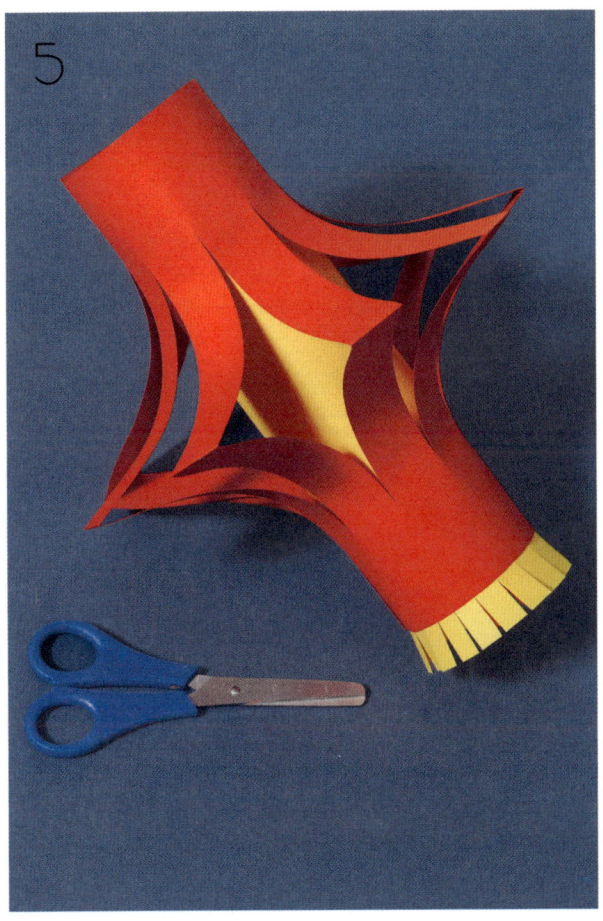

Cut slits at 1 cm intervals into the yellow paper sticking out of the red tube to make a decorative fringe.

6

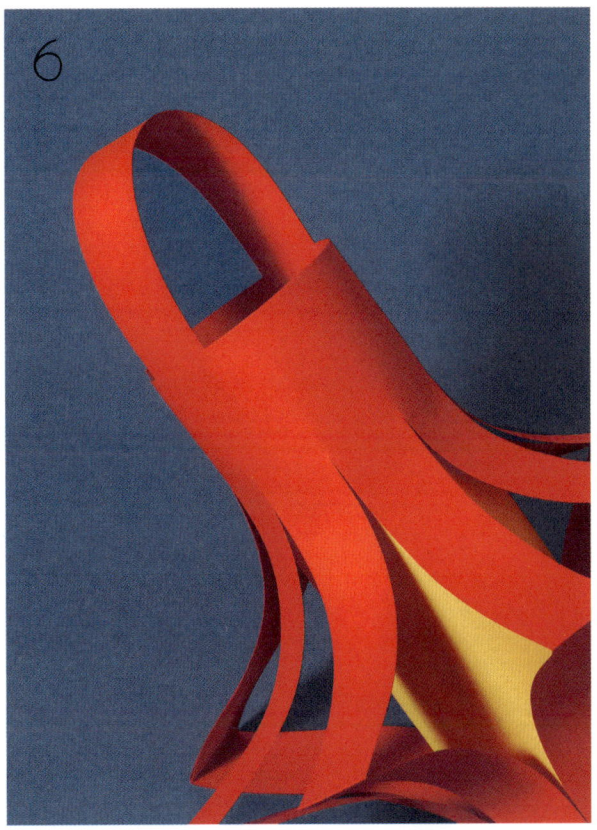

Make a handle for your lantern. Cut a 2 cm wide strip from a piece of red paper. Use double-sided tape to attach the ends of the strip to the top of the red tube. Now hang up your paper lantern for everyone to see.

## Try this!

Why not make lanterns out of paper bags? Sketch a design on a paper bag with pencil, and colour it in with black paint. Put an LED tea light inside the bag and watch your lantern glow.

# Illustrated initials

## Medieval illuminated manuscripts

## Look at this!

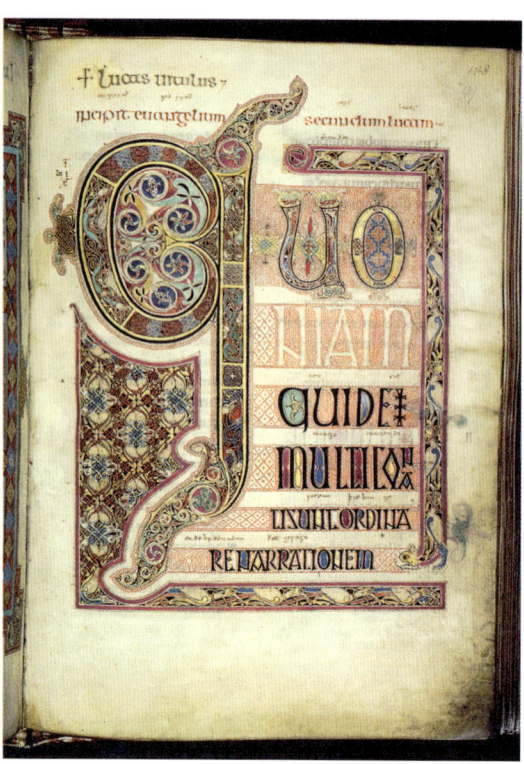

Before the printing press was invented, medieval scribes used ink and quill pens to copy passages from the Bible onto paper. Then they would illuminate – or decorate – the manuscripts with colourful pictures and borders.

St Luke incipit page, Lindisfarne Gospels, c. 700 CE

## Discuss this!

Many Bibles in the medieval period (476–1450 CE) were written in Latin. Most people in the medieval period could not read Latin, but they could understand pictures. That is one reason why churches have statues and stained glass windows showing scenes from the Bible.

• Look at the page from the Lindisfarne Gospels. Do you recognise any of the letters?

• Can you see the animals hiding in the illustrations? There is a cat and a snake. What else can you spot?

• Think about your favourite book. Does it have pictures?

Give it a go!

It's your turn to draw and decorate a letter in the style of an illuminated page.

## You will need:

- White paper
- Ruler
- Pencil
- Coloured pencils
- Gold and silver glitter glue

1

Use a ruler and pencil to draw a 3 cm border around the edge of the paper.

2

Use a pencil to write the first letter of your name in the middle of the page.

3

Decorate your letter by drawing some of your favourite animals, plants, foods, toys or patterns on and around it.

4

Colour in your decorated letter with coloured pencils.

Top tip! Medieval scribes would decorate almost every space on a page. Fill as much of your paper as possible with pictures and colour.

**5**

Fill in the border with a pattern or more of your favourite things. Start with pencil outlines, then colour them in when you are happy with the design.

**6**

Finally, add gold and silver glitter glue to your design to give it an extra-special sparkle.

 Try this!

Complete your training as a scribe by practising medieval handwriting. Copy the letters on this scroll and write your name in medieval style. Scribes would copy for hours and hours to perfect their handwriting.

# Pinched clay pots

Japanese raku pottery

 Look at this!

Raku teabowl, Japan, c. 1840

This Japanese teabowl has been pushed and pulled into shape by hand. It was glazed and fired in a hot kiln, then cooled down quickly. This causes little holes and cracks to appear on the bowl's surface and its glaze to turn interesting colours. These teabowls were used in traditional tea ceremonies. The pot is meant to show the beauty of simple, everyday things

### Discuss this!

Raku teabowls might look a bit wonky, but every piece is unique and full of character.

• Do the patterns on the pot remind you of anything? Perhaps an animal's fur or a map of the world?

• Do you have a favourite cup that you like to drink from?

• Traditional tea ceremonies in Japan are a way of welcoming guests into a home. Have you ever thrown a tea party for your friends?

Give it a go!

It's your turn to make a unique pinched clay pot.

## you will need:

- Air-dry clay
- Small bowl of water
- Modelling tools
- Watercolour paints and paintbrush (optional)

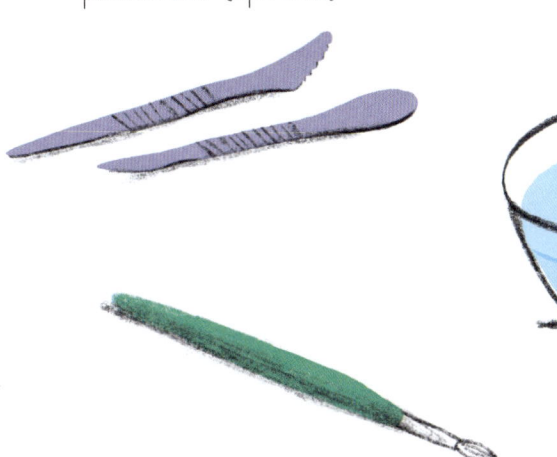

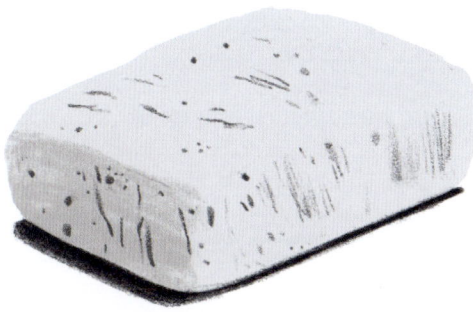

1

Take a piece of air-dry clay large enough to fit in one hand. Roll it between your hands to make a ball.

2

Press your thumb into the middle of the ball to start shaping the pot. Be careful not to push all the way through.

3

Dip your fingertips in water and use your wet fingers to pinch and smooth the clay into a bowl shape.

4

Use modelling tools to decorate your pot with lines, dots and grooves.

**Top tip!** If you accidentally make a hole in the pot, just take a small amount of clay and smooth it over the hole with wet fingers.

Leave your pot in a warm, dry place for 2-3 days, until the clay hardens.
Once the pot is dry, paint it with watercolour paints, or leave it as it is.

REMEMBER: Most air-dry clays are not safe to put food in.
Your pot should only be used as a decoration.

Try this!

Kintsugi is a Japanese pottery technique where cracked or broken pottery is repaired with sticky resin mixed with gold dust. The cracks are not hidden, but shine beautifully. If your clay pinch pot cracks or breaks, stick it back together with PVA glue, and cover the joins with gold paint to give it the Kintsugi look.

# Printed paper

## William Morris's patterned wallpaper

 Look at this!

In 1883 the artist and designer William Morris spotted a bird stealing fruit from his kitchen garden. He was inspired to create one of his most popular print designs: *The Strawberry Thief*. This design was printed onto wallpaper by hand using carved wooden blocks dipped into coloured ink. The process was very time-consuming and took days to complete.

William Morris, *The Strawberry Thief* wallpaper design, 1883

## Discuss this!

Whether he was designing fabrics, furniture or stained-glass windows, William Morris always found inspiration in nature.

• How many birds, flowers, leaves and fruits can you see in *The Strawberry Thief* design?

• Look out of your window. Can you see any plants or animals? What are they doing?

• What are your favourite plants or animals? Do you have any pictures of them in your home?

 Give it a go!

Have a go at making wrapping paper using block printing.

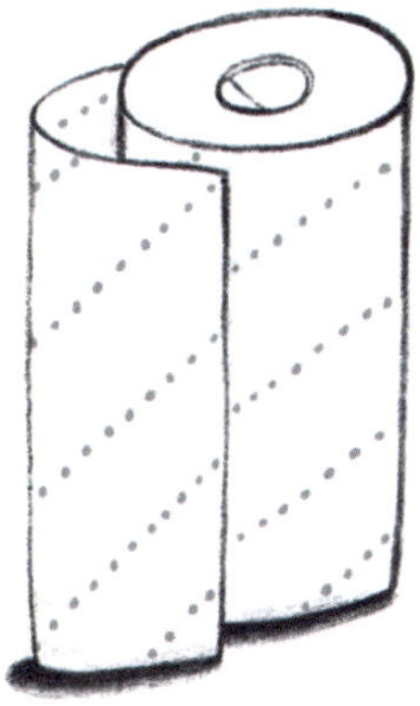

## You will need:

- Large potatoes (one potato makes two stamps)
- Child-safe craft knife or butter knife
- Paper kitchen towel
- Black felt-tip pen
- Large sheet of kraft paper
- Small bowls or plates
- Washable paints in different colours

1

Ask an adult to help you cut your potatoes in half. Blot the cut sides dry with a kitchen towel.

2

Draw one simple shape - such as a star or a leaf - on each cut side of the potato halves with black felt-tip pen.

3

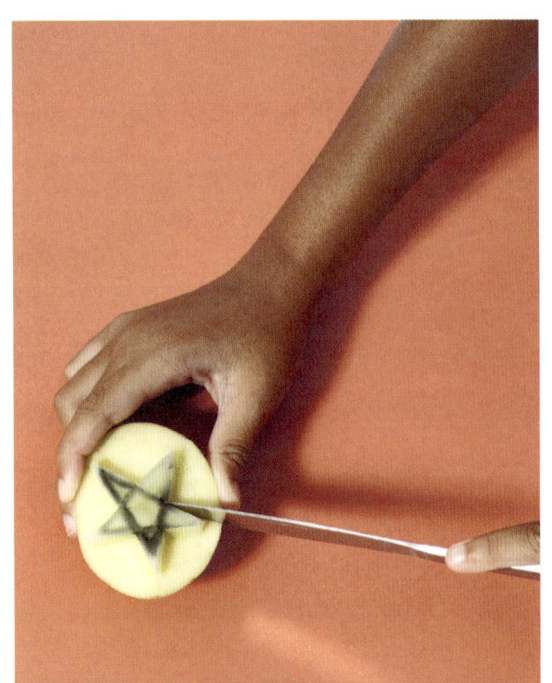

Ask an adult to help you cut away the potato from around the edge of your shape, so that the shape sticks out by about 1.5 cm. Repeat with the other potatoes to make a set of stamps.

4

Put a large sheet of kraft paper flat on a table, and squirt acrylic paints into small plates or bowls that you can dip your stamps in.

5

6

Dip your first stamp in a colour. Press it firmly on the kraft paper, then lift it up to reveal the stamped design. Repeat with the same stamp as many times as you want. Then dip a new stamp in a new colour and go again!

When you are happy with your design, leave your wrapping paper to dry.

**Top tip!** Overlap your different stamps and colours. Always start with light colours before dark ones when layering coloured paints.

## Try this!

If you like printing with potatoes, give printing with leaves a go. Collect some interesting leaves when you are out and about. Wash and dry them, then use a paintbrush to cover them in coloured paint. Press the leaf, paint-side down, onto a sheet of paper. Slowly peel the leaf off the paper and let the paint dry.

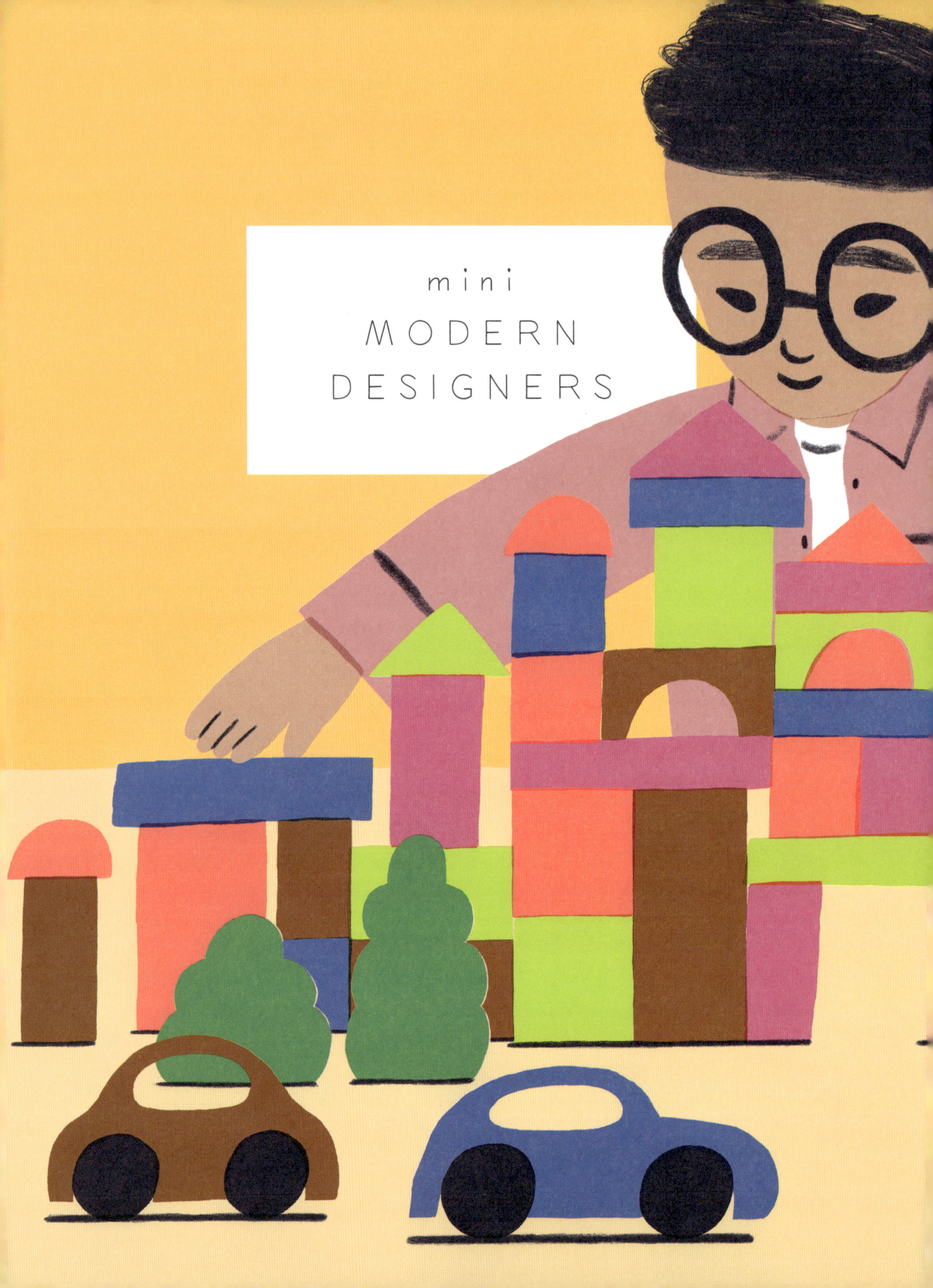

mini
MODERN
DESIGNERS

From mapping out train tracks to designing elegant furniture or creating record-breaking race cars, designers in the 20th century helped to make life easier in a fast-changing world.

Modern design is often well made, practical and easy to use. But it is still full of artistic vision. There is plenty of colour, fun and excitement to be found. In these projects, mini designers will explore Bruno Munari's idea of 'design without purpose' and have a chance to create their own toys, puppets and mobiles.

# Fantastical cities

## London Underground map

 Look at this!

Harry Beck, *Presentation drawing for diagrammatic Underground map*, 1931

Harry Beck designed this map in 1931 to help people find their way around on the London Underground railway (also known as the Tube). The coloured dots show every station that was open when this map was created, and the coloured train lines connect them together.

### Discuss this!

Beck used a lot of straight lines in his design. It makes the map neat and easy to read.

- Can you count how many railway lines there are? How many stations?

- Find a modern London Tube map and look at it next to Beck's. How many new lines and stations can you see?

- Do you know any other cities with underground trains, such as the Paris Metro, or the New York subway? Can you find a map of one of those to look at?

# Give it a go!

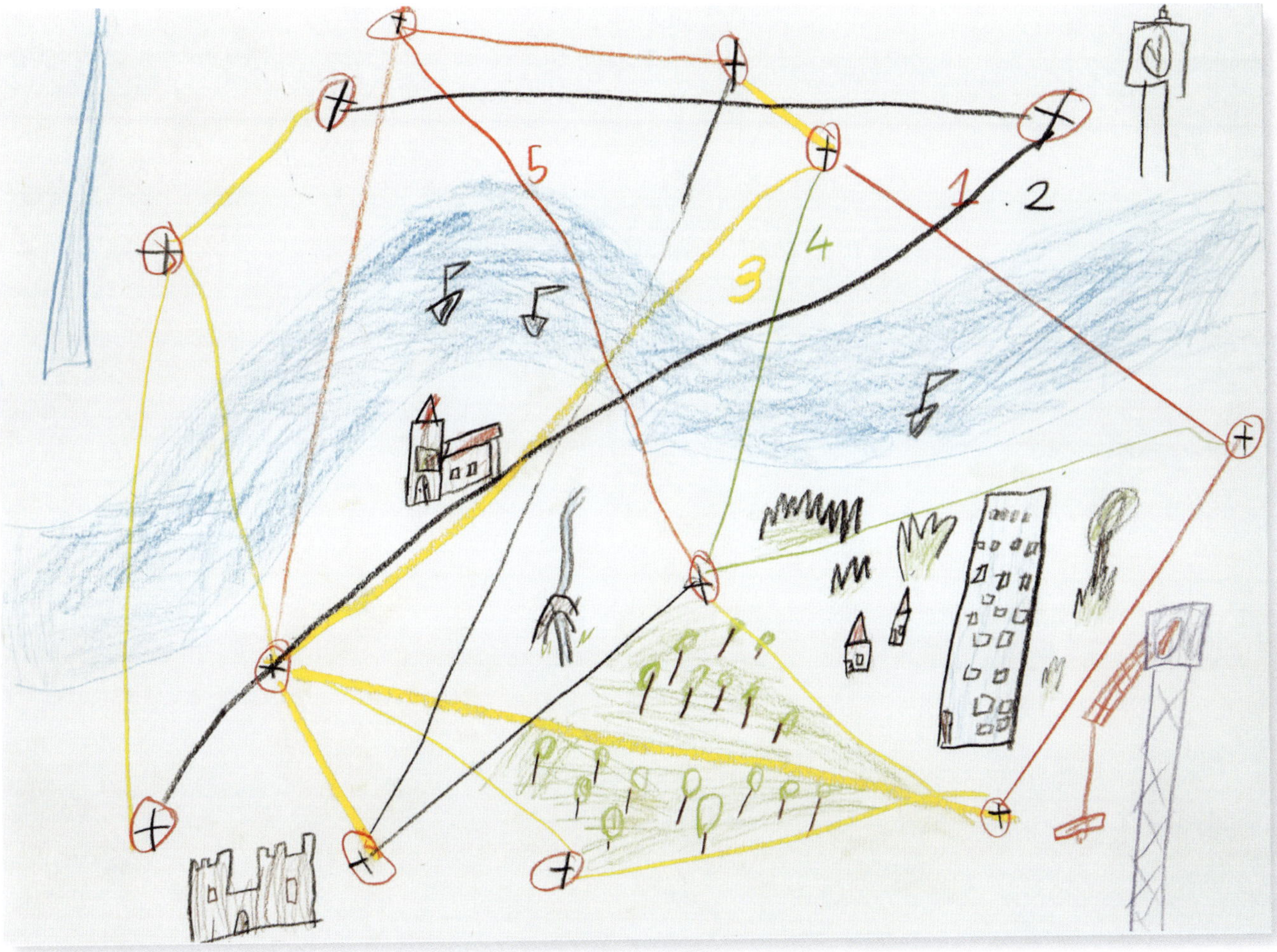

Design your own city map with an underground train system.

## You will need:

- White paper
- Coloured pens or pencils
- Ruler

1

Use a blue pencil to draw a river across the middle of your paper. Will it be straight or have lots of curves and bends?

2

Draw small circles on your map to mark the locations of your train stations. To create your first railway line, use a coloured pencil and a ruler to draw straight lines connecting some of your stations together.

3

Use three or four different colours to draw more railway lines connecting your stations. Remember that stations can connect to more than one railway line. Will you give your railway lines names?

4

Draw some landmarks on your map. Your city could have a castle, a zoo or even a rocket launchpad! Make sure they are close to the stations so that travellers in your city can visit the landmarks easily.

**Top tip!** Spread your stations and landmarks across the entire map to make your city feel big and full of things for visitors to do.

5

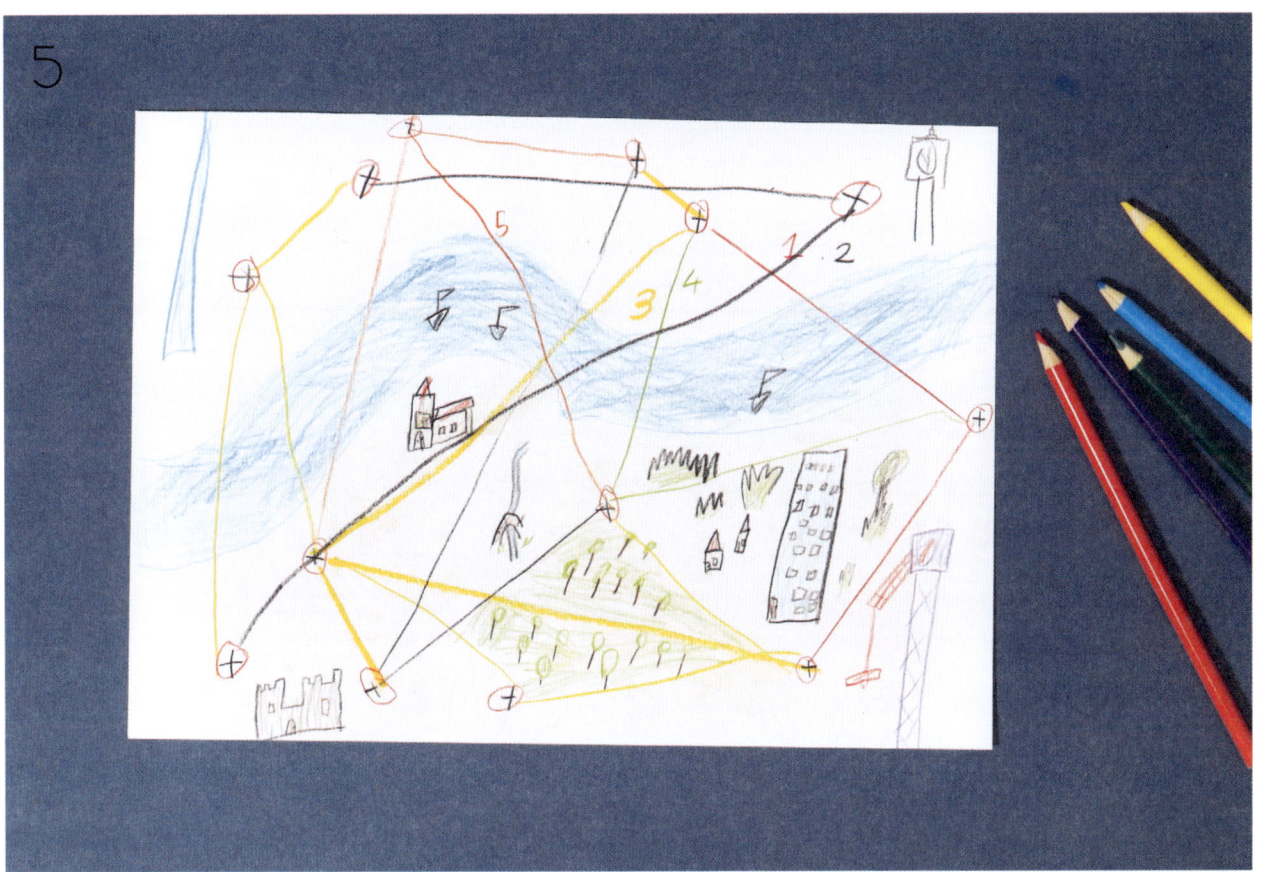

Now your city map is ready to use! Pick two landmarks on your map and work out how to get from one to the other using your railway system. How many stations would you travel through? Do you have to change to a new railway line to reach your destination?

## Try this!

If you like making maps, what about a treasure map? Scrunch up a sheet of white paper, then spread it flat again. Wet a teabag with warm water, then brush and dab the teabag over the paper to turn it brown. When it has dried, the paper will look like an old piece of parchment. Draw some trees, rivers and obstacles such as quicksand or crocodiles, then mark the spot where the treasure is buried with a big X.

# Lollipop loungers

Marsan lounge chair

## Look at this!

Charlotte Perriand, *Low Easy Chair* for Hotel La Cachette, France, c. 1960s

This chair was designed by architect and furniture maker Charlotte Perriand, for the Hotel La Cachette at a ski resort in the French Alps. It came with fabric cushions for extra comfort, so it was a great place to sit and rest after an active day on the slopes.

## Discuss this!

Different types of chair are used for different activities, such as working, chatting, relaxing and even sleeping.

• Do you think this chair looks comfortable? Would you like to sit on it?

• Can you name some different types of seats? A stool, a bench, an armchair... what else?

• Do you have a favourite chair?

# Give it a go!

It's your turn to make
a mini lounge chair
for your toys to enjoy.

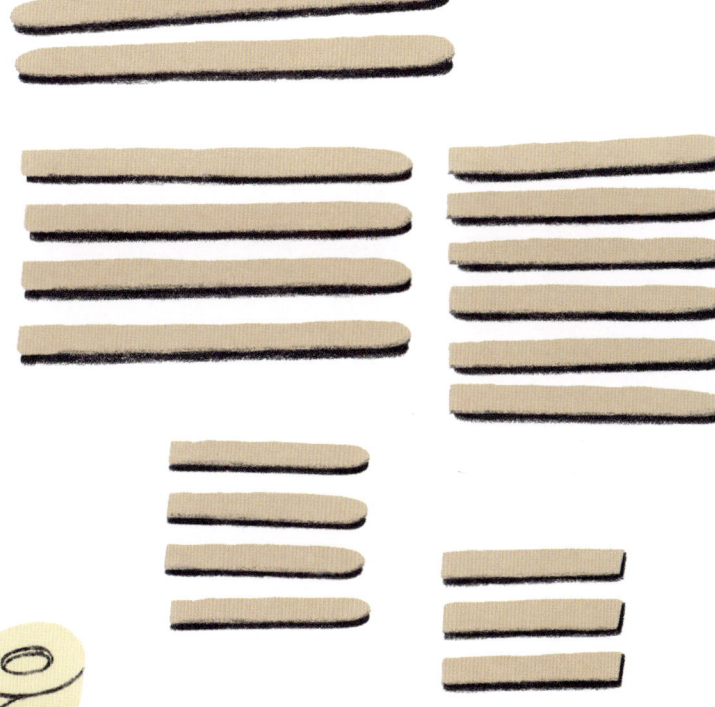

# You will need:

· 20 lollipop sticks, cut to size. Some will need
the round sides to be cut flat. Ask an adult
to cut the sticks before you begin:
> Two 10 cm sticks
> Four 9 cm sticks, with one flat end each
> Six 6 cm sticks, with one flat end each
> Four 4 cm sticks, with one flat end each
> Three 4 cm sticks, both ends flat
· Double-sided tape

1

Use double-sided tape to attach two 10 cm lollipop sticks and two 4 cm sticks together to make a rectangular frame. Attach the shorter sticks 1 cm in from each end of the longer sticks, as shown.

2

To make the seat of your lounge chair, tape four 9 cm sticks flat on top of the frame, keeping the cut ends in line with one of the shorter edges of the frame.

3

To make the chair's backrest, use double-sided tape to stick a 4 cm stick flat across four 6 cm sticks. Tape one 6 cm stick to each edge of the 4 cm stick, as shown.

4

Tape the backrest at a slightly slanted angle to the 1 cm stick ends on the base.

Top tip! You can use PVA glue instead of tape to make your lounge chair stronger. You'll have to be patient and wait for every join to dry between each step.

5

Finally, give your lounge chair some legs. Tape the
flat end of each of the remaining four 4 cm sticks
to the four corners of the base, so the rounded ends
point down. Now the chair can stand up and is ready
for your toys to relax on.

## Try this!

If you enjoy creating toy furniture,
make some egg carton chairs. Cut
out one section of the egg carton.
Ask an adult to snip the sharp
ends off four toothpicks. Glue
or tape the toothpicks to the
bottom of the carton section
to make legs. Use acrylic
paints to colour in your
egg carton chair.

# Mini motorcars

Ferrari racing car

## Look at this!

Model Ferrari 156 F1 'Sharknose' at 1:8 scale, 1961

This elegant car was built by the company Ferrari in 1961. It is
4 metres long with a smooth, pointed front, to help the car drive faster.
The bottom of this car is much lower to the ground than most cars.
This stops the car from wobbling and shaking when it reaches speeds
of up to 260 km per hour – fast enough to win five Grand Prix races!

## Discuss this!

Some people thought the front of the
car looked like a shark with big nostrils,
so it was nicknamed 'Sharknose'.

• Does this car remind you of
a shark? Or of any other animal?

• What other features does the Ferrari
have that make it look different from
regular cars?

• Do you enjoy racing with your friends?
Running, or on a bike or a
scooter perhaps?

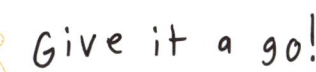 Give it a go!

It's your turn to make a toy race car from cardboard.

# You will need:

- Recycled cardboard tubes
- Coloured paper or card
- Glue stick
- Pencil
- Scissors
- Black felt-tip pen

1

Measure and cut out a rectangle of coloured paper large enough to wrap around the cardboard tube. Glue the coloured paper onto the tube.

2

Use a pencil to draw a semicircle onto the tube with the flat side about 2 cm from one edge. Ask an adult to help you cut around the curved part of the semicircle, then fold it upwards along the straight edge so it sticks up.

3

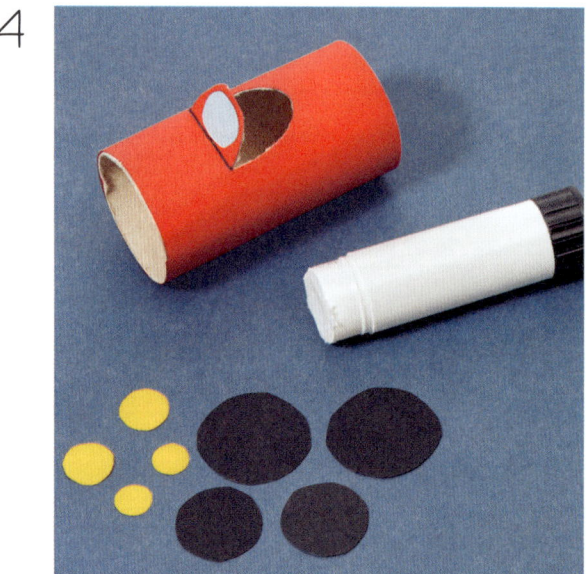

Draw and cut out from paper: two large black circles for the back wheels, two slightly smaller black circles for the front wheels, four yellow circles to fit inside the wheels as hubcaps and one blue oval for the windshield.

4

Glue the blue oval to the front of the windshield flap.

**Top tip!** Why not add a paper steering wheel or even a bumper to accessorise your car?

5

6

Glue the yellow hubcaps to the middle of the black wheels. Then glue the wheels to the sides of your car, with the larger wheels at the back.

Use a black felt-tip pen to draw an outline around the windshield and to decorate the car with some racing stripes and your lucky number on the side. Now you're ready to race!

## Try this!

Organise a race for your toy cars and make a chequered flag to wave at the finish line. Use a ruler and pencil to draw a grid of squares onto a sheet of white paper. Colour in every other square with a black felt-tip. Then stick your flag to a piece of dowel or a lollipop stick and give it a wave.

# Hanging mobile

## Bruno Munari's *Useless Machines*

## Look at this!

Bruno Munari, *Useless Machine*, 1951

Italian designer Bruno Munari thought that the increasing use of machines in the 20th century was a threat to creativity in design. He started designing 'useless machines', with parts that move but – unlike most machines – do not produce or achieve anything.

## Discuss this!

As a child, Munari liked to throw strips of paper in the air and watch how they floated to the ground. These memories inspired him to design light mobiles that move freely in the air.

• Munari's *Useless Machine* uses lots of shapes. Can you name any of them?

• Munari painted the parts of his *Useless Machine* in bright colours. What colours can you see?

• The *Useless Machine* is made of very light materials, so it can move easily. How would you make it move? By touching it? Or perhaps blowing on it?

# Give it a go!

Have a go at designing
a hanging mobile
inspired by Munari's
*Useless Machine.*

## You will need:

• 3 thick paper straws
• 2 white foam or paper balls
• Black paint
• Paint pot
• Paintbrush
• Coloured card
• Pencil
• Scissors
• String
• Sticky tape

Paint patterns on the foam or paper balls with black paint. You could try painting half of one ball and a stripe on the other.

Draw a rectangle, a triangle and a diamond on different coloured card. Cut out the three shapes.

Cut five pieces of string. They don't have to all be the same length. Tape one piece of string to each of the coloured shapes and balls.

Tie the pieces of string to different points along the straws, so the balls and shapes hang down from them. You can hang as many shapes from each straw as you want. When you are happy, tape the string in place.

**Top tip!** Experiment with your mobile by moving the parts to different places.

**5**

**6**

Cut three pieces of string about 8-10 cm long. Tie one piece to the centre of each straw. Arrange your straws in the order you want them to hang, top to bottom. Tie the loose ends of these pieces of string to the centre of the straw above, and tape the string in place. The top piece of string is to hang your mobile.

Use the top piece of string to hang up your finished mobile. Watch how it moves in the air.

## Try this!

Bruno Munari also made sculptures out of paper. Why not make your own? Cut out shapes from a piece of coloured card, then fold the card in half so it stands up. What can you see through the cutouts?

# Split pin puppets

## Charles and Ray Eames' *Colouring Toy*

### Look at this!

Charles and Ray Eames, *Colouring Toy*, 1955

Charles and Ray Eames released the *Colouring Toy* in 1955. The toy contained sheets of shapes, which could be cut out, coloured in and assembled together in lots of different ways. Charles and Ray asked their friend's granddaughter to help design the shapes and the box. Can you imagine being asked to help make a toy?

### Discuss this!

The toy included a doll, a castle and animal shapes, and even a flying dinosaur!

• Look at the parts included with the colouring toy. What shapes can you see?

• Can you see the tiny pencils that came with the toy? How many are there?

• If you were asked to help design a toy, what would you create?

# Give it a go!

Have a go at making puppets from cutout parts.

## You will need:

- White card
- Pencil
- Coloured felt-tip pens
- Scissors
- Split pins
- Sticky tape
- Lollipop sticks

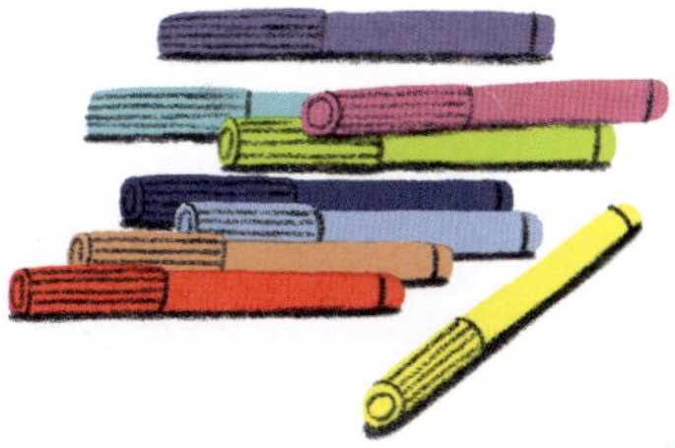

1

Decide what sort of person or creature puppet you want to make. On a sheet of white card, draw their body, head, arms, legs and any other parts, such as a tail. Draw each part separately from each other.

2

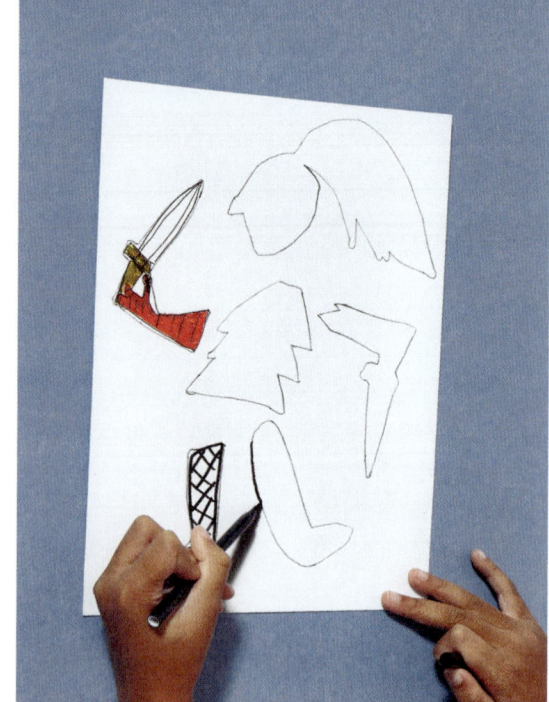

Colour in the puppet's body parts with felt-tips.

3

Cut out each of the puppet's body parts.

4

Push a split pin through the top of one of the puppet's arms. Find the place where you want to attach it to the body and push the pin through there too.

**Top tip!** Use a pencil to mark the places on the puppet where the split pins should be pushed through.

**5**

Fold out the split pin to secure it at the back of the puppet's body. Repeat steps 4-5 with the rest of the puppet's body parts.

**6**

Finally, use sticky tape to attach a lollipop stick to the puppet's back.

## Try this!

Create a theatre box for your puppets. Open up the top and bottom flaps of a cardboard box, then push and fold them flat inside the box. Decorate the box, inside and out, to make a beautiful stage. You could even add some tissue paper curtains to the front. Stand your box theatre on a table and put on a puppet show.

# Eye-catching images

*Children Crossing* road sign

 Look at this!

The *Children Crossing* road sign was designed by Margaret Calvert and Jock Kinneir for UK roads in the 1950s and 60s. Calvert based the child on the right of the sign on an image of herself as a child. Sometimes you don't need to look far to find inspiration.

Margaret Calvert and Jock Kinneir, *Children Crossing* sign for British roadways, 1957-1967

## Discuss this!

Simple pictures that deliver messages are called pictograms. Different shaped road signs are for different types of message. Circles give orders, triangles warn you about something and rectangles give information.

- What do you think the *Children Crossing* sign is for? Where do you think you would see it?

- What signs do you see when you are out and about? Do you know what they mean?

- Road signs need to catch people's attention quickly. Why do you think Margaret Calvert and Jock Kinneir chose red and black for their designs?

# Give it a go!

It's your turn to design an eye-catching sign.

# You will need:

- White paper
- Black and red felt-tip pens
- Pencil
- Scissors

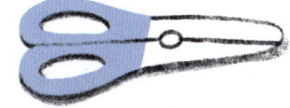

1

Decide if your sign will give orders (circle), a warning (triangle) or information (rectangle). Use a red felt-tip pen to draw the outline of your shape on white paper.

2

Colour in a thick border around your shape with red felt-tip pen.

3

Sketch your pictogram message inside your sign with a pencil. Maybe you want to warn people about monsters, or stones falling off a cliff. Be creative!

4

Colour in your pictogram with black felt-tip pen.

Top tip! Keep your pictogram simple. The simpler it is, the easier for everyone to understand the message quickly.

5

Cut out your road sign with scissors. Stick your sign on your bedroom door to alert your visitors!

Try this!

Design your own traffic lights inspired by the iconic East Berlin Crossing Man (Ampelmännchen). Use a white pencil or chalk to draw an outline of a walking person on a sheet of black paper. Cut the shape out and cover the hole with a sheet of green tissue paper. Repeat this process, but this time draw a standing person and cover the shape with red tissue paper. Hold a torch behind the shapes to see the traffic lights glow!

# Overlapping letters

## Massimo Vignelli's typography posters

### Look at this!

Massimo Vignelli, *Knoll International poster*, 1967

Can you read the word on this poster? It says 'Knoll'. It was designed for the American furniture company Knoll by Massimo Vignelli. The eye-catching colours overlap to create new colours and patterns.

### Discuss this!

Massimo Vignelli used a simple font and only three colours (blue, yellow and pink), but played with the size and space of the letters to make his design.

• Can you see the letter 'K' in the design? What other letters can you see?

• Look at the colours on the poster. What colour is made where pink overlaps with yellow? Or yellow with blue?

• Have you ever mixed different coloured paints to create new colours?

Give it a go!

It's your turn to design a poster with overlapping letters.

# You will need:

- A large sheet of white paper
- Cardboard
- Scissors
- Blue, yellow and pink acrylic paint
- Paper plates.

1

Pick a three-letter word – we used BAM – or you could use your initials. Use scissors to cut out three small, cardboard rectangles. These will be your paint scrapers.

2

Squeeze a blob of each of paint colour onto a paper plate.

3

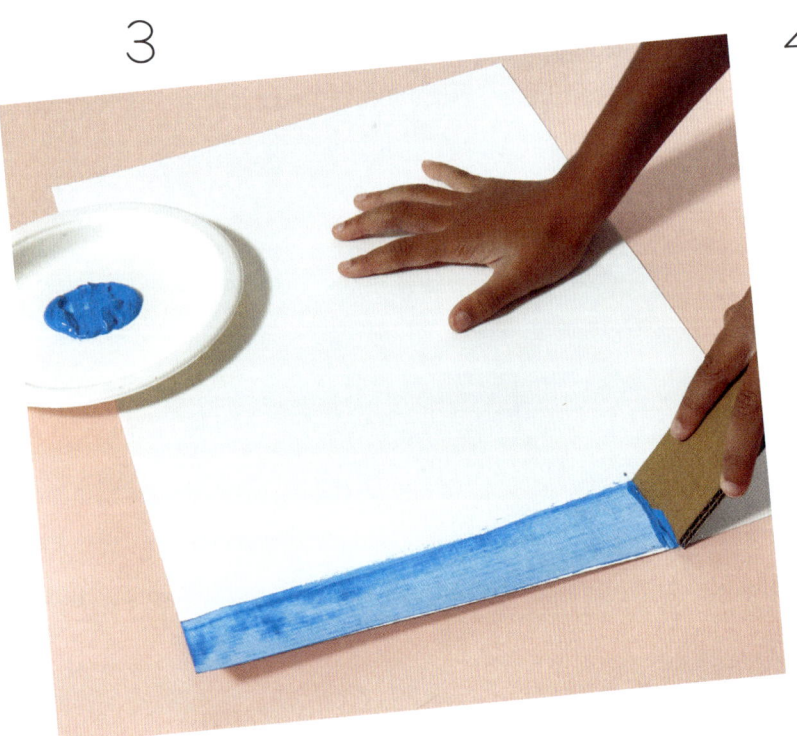

Dip your first cardboard scraper in the blue paint and use it to draw the first letter of your word on the left side of the white paper.

4

Dip your second scraper in the pink paint. Draw the third letter of the word on the right side of the paper. Let the paint dry.

5

6

Use the third paint scraper to paint the middle letter in yellow. Make sure it overlaps with the first and third letters. What new colours are created?

When the paint is dry, stick up your colourful poster for people to see.

**Top tip!** To get the best overlapping effect, it is best to start with blue and pink, which are darker colours, and then layer the lighter yellow on top.

## Try this!

Vignelli designed all sorts of things, including invitations. Design your own cards using scrape painting. Cover a piece of paper in dots of different-coloured acrylic paint. Take a piece of cardboard and scrape the paint across the paper in different directions. When the paint is dry, write your message on the back. Why not use them as party invitations?

mini
CONTEMPORARY
DESIGNERS

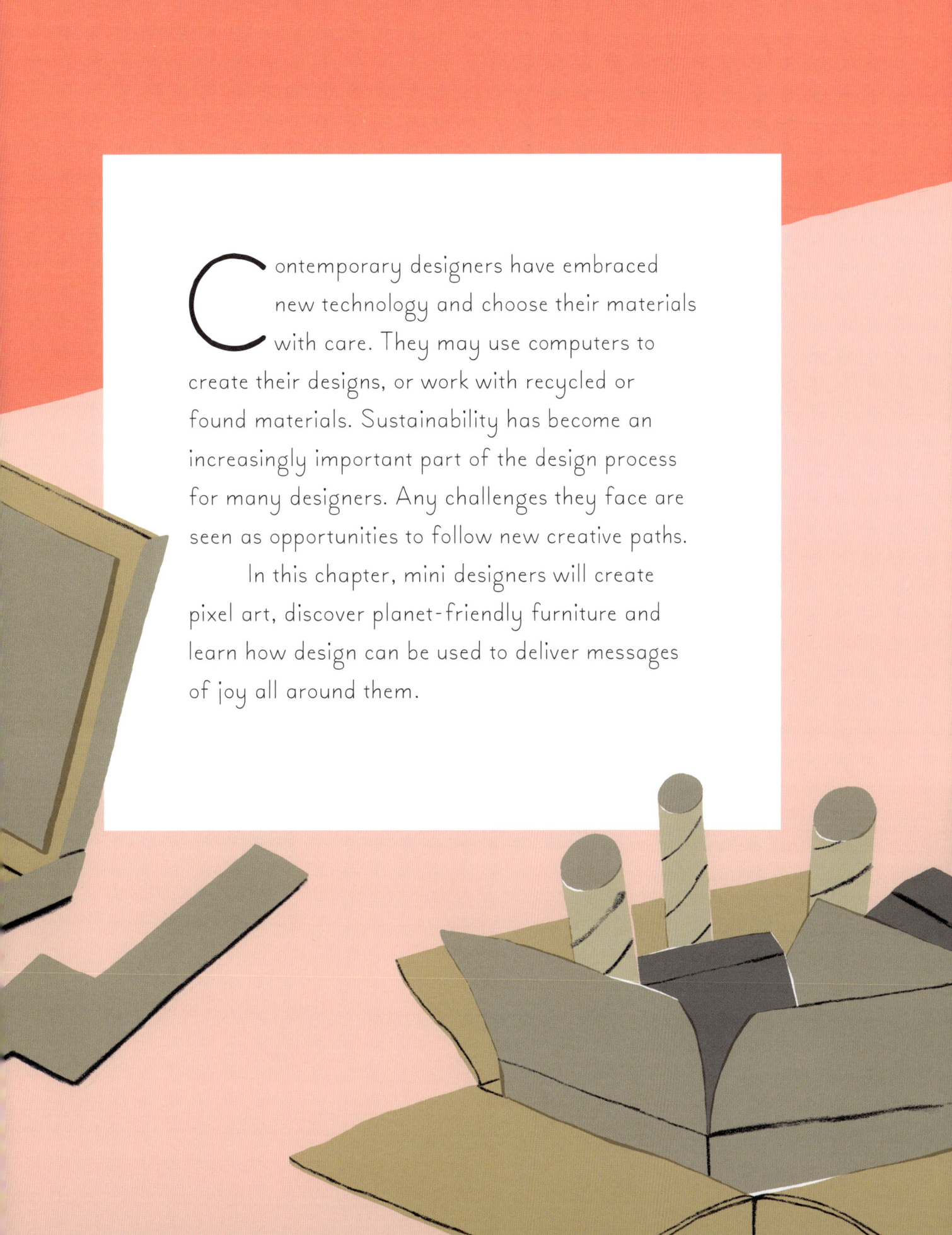

Contemporary designers have embraced new technology and choose their materials with care. They may use computers to create their designs, or work with recycled or found materials. Sustainability has become an increasingly important part of the design process for many designers. Any challenges they face are seen as opportunities to follow new creative paths.

In this chapter, mini designers will create pixel art, discover planet-friendly furniture and learn how design can be used to deliver messages of joy all around them.

# Pixel art creatures

## Susan Kare's Dogcow

**Look at this!**

Graphic designer Susan Kare used a computer to design this cute creature that looks a bit like a dog and a bit like a cow. Susan also designed thousands of computer icons for Apple Macintosh computers in the 1980s, like the Grabber and the Paint Bucket.

Susan Kare, *Dog symbol from the Cairo font*, 1983

**Discuss this!**

Computer screens are divided into grids of tiny squares called pixels. When pixels are filled in with colours, they create a picture.

• Can you think of any other crafts that use squares? What about mosaics? Have you heard of cross-stitch?

• Kare gave her Dogcow a name: Clarus. What name would you give the Dogcow?

• Some icons on a computer make a sound when you click on them. What sound do you think the Dogcow makes (answer below)?

(It says 'Moof!', a combination of 'moo' and 'woof'!)

# Give it a go!

It's your turn to create fantastical animals from tiny squares.

# You will need:

- Squared paper
- Pencil
- Ruler
- Eraser
- Felt-tip pens

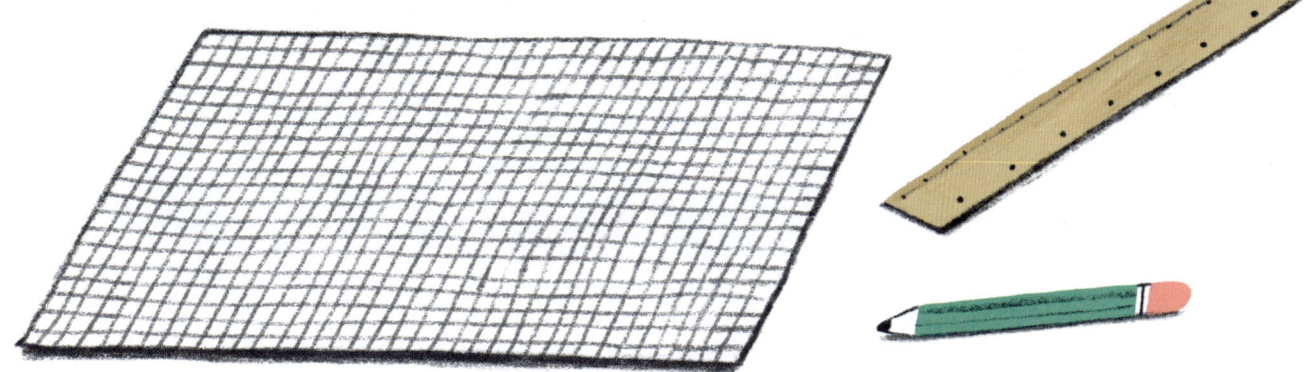

1

First choose two animals to combine
into your design. Pick squared paper
with large squares for a simple design,
or with smaller squares if you want to
include more details.

2

Draw the outline of your creature with
a pencil or black felt-tip pen. Follow the
lines of the squared paper.

3

Draw your creature's eyes, mouth and
other details such as spots or stripes.

4

Colour in your creature with felt-tip pens. Only
use one colour per square, and colour within the
lines on the paper. Susan Kare's Dogcow was
black and white. You can do the same or use
colours. Will you leave any squares white?

**Top tip!** Practise drawing your design with pencil first, before using felt-tip pens.

5

Give your creature design a name. What sound would it make?

## Try this!

Now you know how to make 2D pixel art, have a go at 3D pixel sculptures. Copy this template onto a piece of coloured card, then cut out the shape. Fold along the dotted lines to make a cube and fasten the edges together with sticky tape. Make lots of cubes from coloured card, then stack them together to make a 3D design.

# Stylish tea set

## Marimekko's bold patterns

### Look at this!

The Marimekko design house has been making bold prints for clothes, accessories and ceramics since 1951. This cheerful design was created in 2009 for Marimekko by Maija Louekari and shows beautiful summer flowers that might grow in a garden.

Maija Louekari, *Siirtolapuutarha (City Garden)*, 2009

### Discuss this!

This design is called *Siirtolapuutarha*, which means 'city garden' in Finnish. It was inspired by Maija Louekari's childhood in Finland.

• Louekari uses basic shapes and strong lines and dots to represent nature. Can you spot a sunflower? A cactus? What else?

• Can you imagine walking through a summer garden? What would it smell like? What sounds would you hear?

• Some parts of this design are coloured in, and some are black and white. Which parts do you like best?

## Give it a go!

It's your turn to create a flower-patterned tea set.

## You will need:

- Paper plates or cups
- Pencil
- Paintbrush
- Watercolour paints
- Bowl of water
- Black felt-tip pen

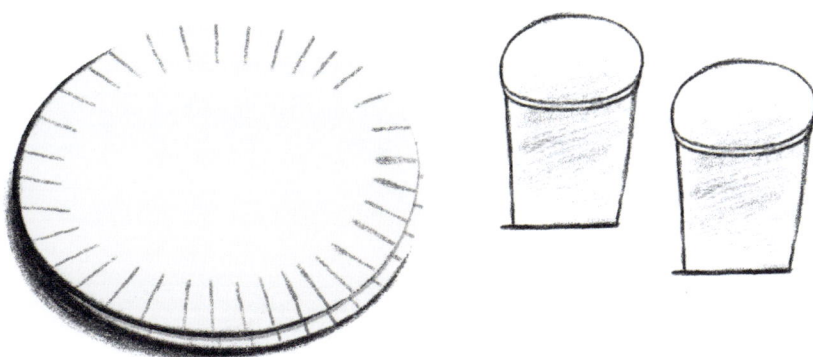

1

Sketch your design in pencil onto a paper plate. Will you include flowers, fruits or vegetables? Use simple shapes. You don't need lots of details.

2

Add some dots and stripes to some of the shapes in your design.

3

Use watercolour paints to colour in your design. Let the paint dry.

4

Draw over your pencil outlines with black felt-tip pen.

**Top tip!** Make sure your paint is not too dark or thick, so you can see the pencil lines underneath.

5

Colour in the dots and stripes with black felt-tip pen. Copy your
design onto more plates and cups to create a matching tea set.

Try this!

Maija Louekari made another
design called *Räsymatto*, with
lots of different coloured dots.
To make your own dotty design,
use a ruler and pencil to draw
straight lines across a sheet of
white paper. Then use coloured
crayons or felt-tip pens to fill in
the lines with lots and lots of dots!

# Patchwork jars

## Hella Jongerius' mixed media vases

 Look at this!

Dutch designer Hella Jongerius combines different materials in her designs. To create these vases, she used a mix of materials including glass, porcelain and packing tape.

Hella Jongerius, Long Neck and Groove Bottles, 2000

## Discuss this!

Take a closer look at the materials and colours in the vases. There is glass and plastic, blue and pink. What else can you see?

- Can you guess what each part is made from? How do you think Hella Jongerius joined the different parts together?

- Do you have any vases in your home? Are they made from glass? Clay? Or maybe plastic?

- What's your favourite colour? Do you like a warm red or a calming blue? Perhaps a striking yellow? Does your favourite colour sometimes change?

# Give it a go!

It's time to design your own mixed-up vase using new and recycled materials.

# You will need:

- Modelling clay in different colours
- Rolling pin
- Recycled glass jars, cleaned and dried
- Washi tapes in different colours
- Scissors

Use a rolling pin to roll and squash stripes of coloured modelling clay together into a band long enough to wrap around the jar, and a little wider than half of the jar's height.

Wrap the clay band around the top half of the jar, with 4-5 cm of clay sticking up from the top.

Pinch and shape the top of the clay around your finger to create the neck of your vase.

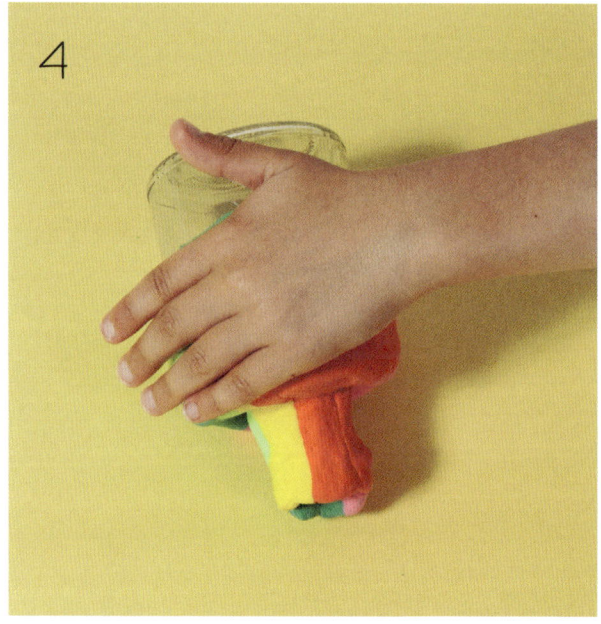

Roll the jar over a flat surface to make the clay smooth.

**Top tip!** Use brightly coloured clay and washi tape with fun patterns to give your vase contrast.

5

Wrap washi tape around the bottom edge of the clay to fix it to the jar and create a neat edge.

6

Decorate the vase with more washi tape stripes. When you are happy with your design, display your vase on a table or windowsill and fill it with flowers.

## Try this!

Make some flowers to fill your vase. Using a pipe cleaner as a stem, twist coloured tissue paper squares around one end of the pipe cleaner to form petals. Fasten them in place with washi tape. Mix materials like Hella Jongerius - stick a pom-pom or a dried autumn leaf to a pipe cleaner.

# Recycled tower

Brunno Jahara's fruit stands

## Look at this!

Brunno Jahara, *Multiplástica Doméstica*, *Fruit stand*, 2013

Brazilian product designer Brunno Jahara recycles plastic objects to make something beautiful out of things that would otherwise have been thrown away. This is an example of working sustainably. This tower - designed to display fruit - is colourful, cool...and good for the planet!

## Discuss this!

Jahara always uses different combinations of objects, colours and shapes when he designs his fruit towers.

• Look at each part of the tower. What types of fruit would you put at the bottom? What would you put at the top?

• Does the shape of the tower remind you of anything? What about a fountain?

• Have you given away clothes you don't wear anymore, or toys you don't play with? Has anyone gifted you something that they don't use anymore?

Give it a go!

It's your turn to make a layered fruit display tower out of recycled objects.

## You will need:

- Old bowls, cups and plates (the more colourful, the better)
- Old plastic toys and sports equipment (such as a badminton shuttlecock)
- Double-sided tape or sticky tack

1

Gather objects to make your tower:
a large bowl, a plastic plate, paper
cups and old container lids. What about
some toys or sports equipment? Wash
anything that isn't made of paper or
card with warm, soapy water.

2

Pick the largest, widest object to be the
base of your fruit stand. A wide bowl
or plate will work best.

3

Make the tower's central column. Stack
tall, thin objects such as cups together,
with container or jar lids in between. Place
the column in the middle of your base.

4

Add a plastic plate that is wide
and flat enough to hold some fruit,
about halfway up your tower.

**Top tip!** Balance is key in this project. If the tower looks a bit wobbly,
take it apart and try a different order.

**5**

Finish building your tower, using smaller objects the higher you build. When you are happy with the height and order of your design, use double-sided tape or sticky tack to fix every object securely in place.

**6**

Decorate your tower with fruit. Put the largest and heaviest fruits on the bottom layer and smaller, lighter ones closer to the top. Or you could display sweets or small cakes. Time for a tea party!

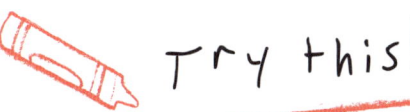 Try this!

Rinse out an empty 2-litre plastic bottle and ask an adult to cut it in half, and to poke some drainage holes in the bottom of the lower half. Paint a cute animal face design on the bottom half of the bottle. You could even cut out some ear shapes. Fill it with soil and place a small house plant into it. Water your plant and watch it grow in your recycled planter.

# Yarn coasters

Simone Post's recycled fabric creations

 Look at this!

Simone Post uses scraps of fabric left over from textile factories to make carpets. The circular designs are inspired by the side view of a rolled-up carpet. Simone believes that experimenting with different ideas whilst designing makes the final product more interesting.

Simone Post, *Vlisco Recycled Carpet - #28*

## Discuss this!

Sometimes the waste left behind after creating things can be recycled into something new. It's much better than just throwing it away.

• Does the carpet's design remind you of anything? What about a target? Or a yummy Swiss roll cake?

• How many colours can you see in the carpet? How many different pieces do you think it was made from?

• Do you have any leftover materials from other craft projects? What interesting new things could you make with them?

# Give it a go!

It's your turn to make a spiralling fabric coaster.

## You will need:

- Felt
- Scissors
- Two balls of chunky, coloured yarn
- Measuring tape or ruler
- Sticky tape
- PVA glue
- Glue pot
- Glue spreader or brush

1

Use a measuring tape or ruler to measure and cut a 1 metre (100 cm) strand from each ball of yarn.

2

Lie the yarn strands next to each other. Find one end of each strand and stick them together with sticky tape, as shown.

3

Cover the whole felt square in PVA glue.

4

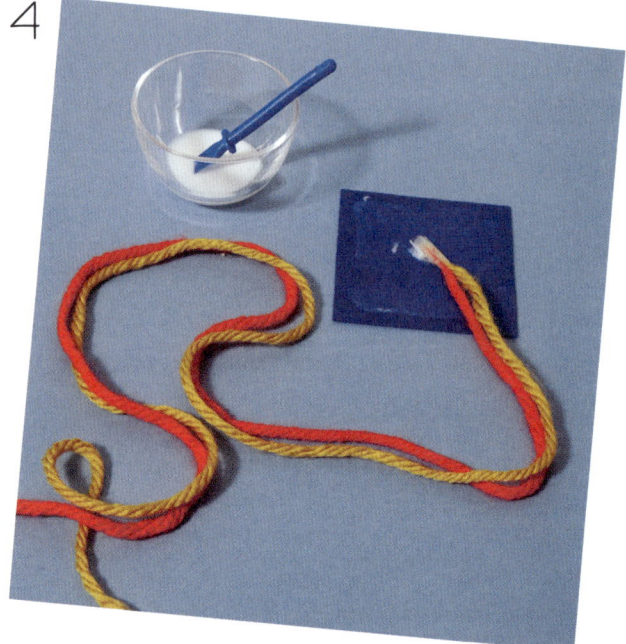

Stick the taped ends of the yarn strands in the middle of the felt square.

**Top tip!** To make a new pattern, twist your yarn strands together, or add a third yarn strand and plait them together. What colour combinations can you make?

5

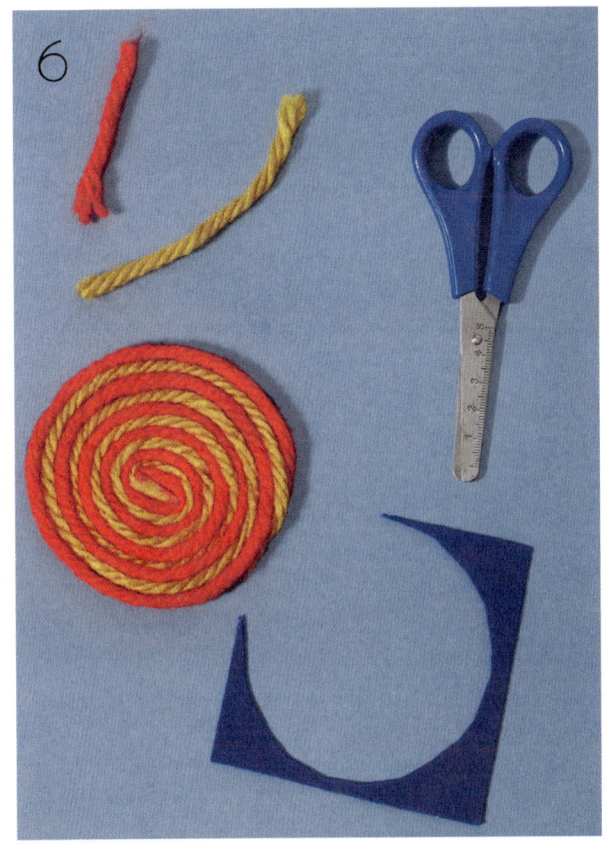

6

Working from the middle of the felt square, start sticking both yarn strands down next to each other in a spiral shape, moving outwards towards the edges of the felt. Make sure the yarn strands do not twist together as you glue them down. Add more PVA glue if you need to. When the yarn spiral reaches the edge of the felt square, stop and let the glue dry.

Cut off any excess yarn and any felt from around the edge of your yarn coaster. Save the cut-off material for a future craft!

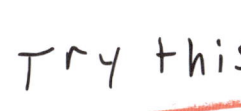

## Try this!

Simone Post tested how different colour combinations of yarn looked by making colour control sticks. Why not create your own colour control sticks by picking two or three colours of yarn and twisting them around a length of dowel or a lollipop stick. Which combinations are your favourite? Are you inspired to make a new coaster?

# Super stools

## Jean-Servais Somian's basin seats

 Look at this!

Furniture designer and sculptor Jean-Servais Somian made this comfy-looking stool from a recycled basin topped with a cushion. Somian is inspired by his West African heritage and uses materials made near his home in Grand-Bassam, in the Republic of Côte d'Ivoire.

Jean-Servais Somian, *Tabouret Bassine*, 2021

## Discuss this!

Somian recycles laundry basins by turning them upside-down to make his stools.

• Do you like the patterns and colours on the basin and cushion?

• Can you think of other ways to use the basin? What would you turn it into?

• Have you tried using an object for a different purpose to what it was designed for? What about turning a clothes peg into a hair pin, or a paper plate into a fan?

Give it a go!

Design your own comfy and colourful bucket stool.

## You will need:

- Thick, corrugated cardboard (the chunkier the better)
- Black felt-tip pen
- Scissors
- White fabric
- Fabric paint pens
- Large safety pins
- A strong bucket (one with a fun pattern works best)

1

Use the bottom of the bucket to trace a circle on the corrugated cardboard with a black felt-tip pen. Ask an adult to help cut out the circle. This will be your cushion.

2

Put the cardboard circle on top of the white fabric. Measure and cut out enough fabric to wrap all around the circle.

3

Use fabric paint pens to create a bold pattern on the fabric. What colour will you use first?

4

Use the fabric paint pens to cover the fabric with colourful patterns and shapes. When you are happy with your design, leave it to dry.

**Top tip!** If you can't find fabric paint or paint pens, decorate the cardboard circle with felt-tip pens or acrylic paints.

Wrap the decorated fabric around the cardboard circle. Fasten the fabric together with safety pins.

Turn your bucket upside-down and place the colourful cushion on top of it, pinned-side facing down. Doesn't your super stool look comfy? Give it a test!

## Try this!

Jean-Servais Somian's furniture designs are colourful and bold, like this wooden cabinet. Make your own colourful tower by painting the boxes with bright red, blue and yellow paint. Glue the boxes on top of each other. When they are dry, store your toys or craft materials on your colourful shelves.

# Joyful pavements

## Yinka Ilori's colourful murals

### Look at this!

British-Nigerian designer Yinka Ilori brought colour to busy roads by replacing black-and-white striped pedestrian crossings with bright, fun patterns. The *Bring London Together* art project was intended to bring joy to the thousands of people who cross London's streets every day.

Yinka Ilori, *Bring London Together*, Tottenham Court Road, London, UK, 2021

### Discuss this!

Ilori said that colours and patterns are his way of celebrating places, communities and experiences.

• Imagine walking over this crossing. How would it make you feel? Would you smile as you walked over it?

• Could you play a game on this design? What about hopscotch, or a giant game of snakes and ladders?

• Look around your home. Can you spot any of the bright colours used in Ilori's design, like neon green or electric blue?

# Give it a go!

It's your turn to give a pavement a technicolour makeover.

## you will need:

• Painter's tape
• Jumbo chalks

1

Find a clean pavement or pathway to make
your colourful crossing. Use painter's tape
to create a border for your crossing design.

2

Use painter's tape to make smaller shapes
inside the border. Use different types of
shapes – if your border is a square, why
not fill it with triangles?

3

Colour in each small shape with jumbo
chalks. Use your fingers to get colour into
any bumps or cracks.

4

When all the shapes are filled with colour,
pull up the painter's tape to reveal neat lines.

Walk across your colourful crossing. Invite some friends to use it, and even play a game on it. Does it make you smile? Remember to take pictures, as the crossing will wash away when it rains.

**Top tip!** Choose a safe, clean space for your design, away from busy roads, and make sure there is an adult with you when making and using it.

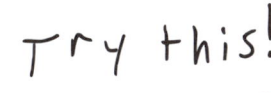 Try this!

Have a go at making murals indoors! All you need is some thick paper, masking tape and paint. Make shapes on your paper using masking tape and colour them in with paint. Wait for the paint to dry before removing the tape. Put it up in a window for passers-by to see.

# List of designs

First published in the United Kingdom in 2025 by Thames & Hudson Ltd, 6-24 Britannia Street, London WC1C 9JD

*Mini Designers* © 2025 Thames & Hudson Ltd, London

Text © 2025 Joséphine Seblon
Illustrations © 2025 Robert Sae-Heng
Photography by Lauren Winsor © 2025 Thames & Hudson Ltd, London
For image reproduction copyright see above

EU Authorized Representative: Interart S.A.R.L.
19 rue Charles Auray, 93500 Pantin, Paris, France
productsafety@thameshudson.co.uk
interart.fr

A CIP catalogue record for this book is available from the British Library

ISBN 978-0-500-66041-6
01

Printed and bound in China by C & C Offset Printing Co. Ltd

Be the first to know about our new releases, exclusive content and author events by visiting
thamesandhudson.com
thamesandhudsonusa.com
thamesandhudson.com.au

A huge thank you to my children and their friends who happily road-tested the projects. And to all the designers out there who make our lives - starting with this book! - so much better. - J.S.

For Plum. A gentle ginger cat whose adventure continues in these books. - R.S.H.